Thumbelina

Illustrated by Eric Kincaid

Once there was a woman who wanted
a child. She went to see a witch.
The witch gave her a barleycorn.
It was a very special barleycorn.

The woman took
the barleycorn
home and planted
it. It grew into
a flower like
a tulip. The
petals were
tightly closed.

The woman kissed
the petals. They
opened. Inside
the flower was
a tiny girl no
bigger than the
woman's thumb. The
woman called the
child Thumbelina.

Thumbelina slept
in a cradle made
from a walnut
shell. The covers
were made from
flower petals.

Thumbelina played
in a boat made
from a tulip
petal.

One day an ugly toad hopped
through the window. The toad
wanted Thumbelina as a wife for
her son. The toad carried the
cradle away. Thumbelina was asleep
inside it.

The toad put the cradle on a lily
leaf. She went to get a room ready
under the mud.
When Thumbelina awoke she was
afraid. Soon the toad came back.
She took the cradle to the room.
She left Thumbelina sitting on the
lily leaf.

The fish did not
like to see
Thumbelina cry.
They nibbled
through the lily
stem. The leaf
floated down the
river. Thumbelina
went with it.

A butterfly pulled
the leaf some of
the way.

A big beetle
picked Thumbelina
up. It took her
to a tree.

The other beetles
thought Thumbelina
was ugly.
"Let her go," they
said.
The beetle put
Thumbelina down on
a daisy.

Thumbelina stayed
in the wood. She
lived by herself.
But she was never
lonely. The birds
were her friends.
Her clothes were
tattered and torn,
but she was never
cold. She was happy
all day long.

Then winter came.
The wind was very
cold. Thumbelina
tried to keep warm.

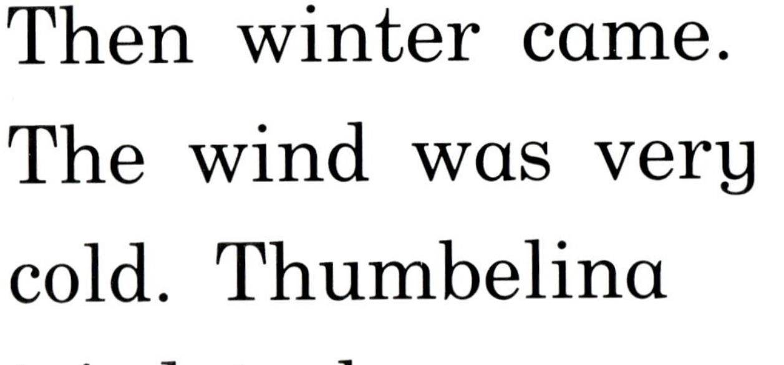

Snow began to fall.
Thumbelina wrapped
herself in a leaf.
If she did not
find somewhere
warm to stay she
would die.

Thumbelina went
into a field where
the corn had been
cut. She knocked
at a door. A field
mouse opened it
and asked her in.
"You can stay with
me as long as you
like," said the
field mouse.

The mole came on
a visit. He said
he would like to
marry Thumbelina.

Thumbelina and the field mouse
went to see the mole's house.
The mole led them along a dark
tunnel. On the way they passed
a swallow. It was lying very still.
"It's dead!" said the mole.
He pushed the swallow with his foot.

Thumbelina could not forget the swallow. She waited until the others were asleep. Then she went back to the tunnel.

She lay her head on the swallow's chest. Its heart was beating.
It was not dead. It had fainted because it was so cold. Thumbelina covered it up to make it as warm as she could.

Thumbelina went back to the
swallow the next night. It had
opened its eyes. Thumbelina looked
after the swallow all winter long.
It grew well and strong.

Spring came. Thumbelina made a hole in the roof of the tunnel. Now the swallow could fly away.

"Sit on my back and I will take you with me," said the swallow. "I cannot," said Thumbelina. "I am to marry the mole." She watched sadly as the swallow flew away.

The wedding day drew near.
Thumbelina sat all day at the
spinning wheel, spinning thread for
her wedding dress. Thumbelina was
unhappy. She did not like the mole.
She did not want to marry him. She
did not want to live underground
for the rest of her life.

It was Thumbelina's
wedding day. The
mole said she
could take one
last look at the
sun. Thumbelina
looked up at the
sky for the last
time. She heard
someone call.
It was the swallow.
"Come, fly with
me!" said the
swallow. This time
Thumbelina did.

The swallow took
Thumbelina to the
place where the
swallows make
their nests.

Near the nests were some white
flowers. Living inside the flowers
were tiny people like herself.

Thumbelina married the King of the
tiny people. She wore a golden
crown. She was given a pair of
wings as a wedding present.
Thumbelina changed her name to
Maia and lived happily ever after.

All these appear in the pages of the story. Can you find them?

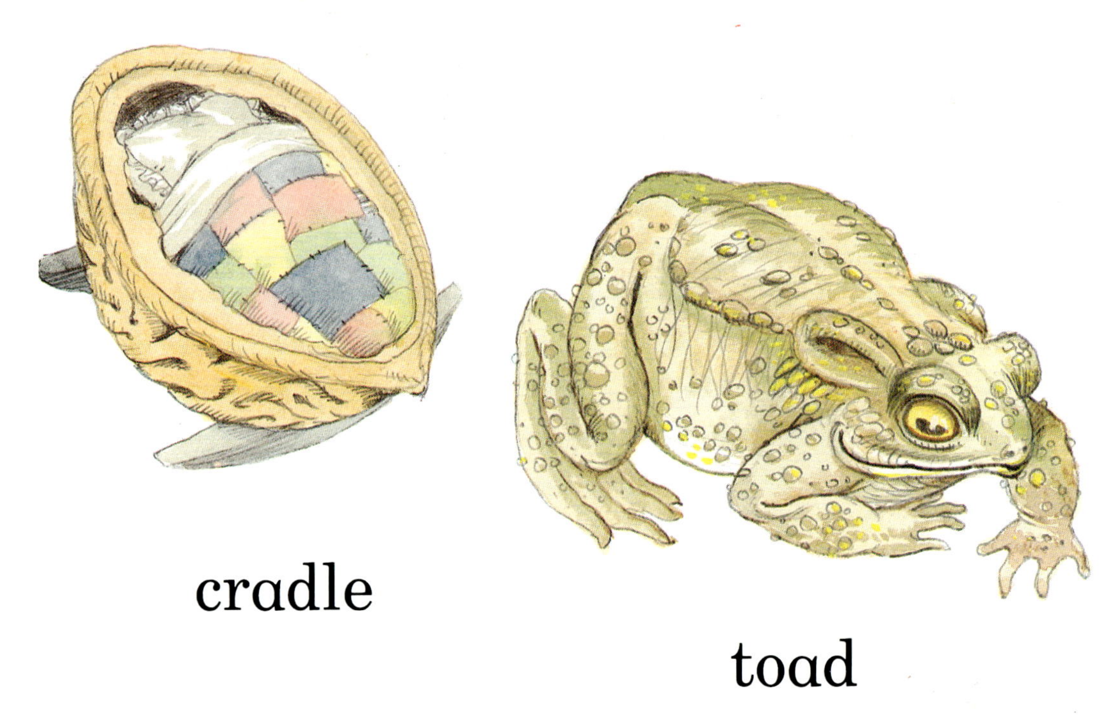

cradle

toad

fish

butterfly